7 Seasons Of Income

To Create And Maintain Wealth

Charles B.Salomon

© **Copyright 2020** by _ Charles B. Salomon _ All rights reserved.

ISBN: 9798562807809

This document is geared towards providing exact and reliable information with regards to the topic and issue covered. The publication is sold with the idea that the publisher is not required to render accounting, officially permitted, or otherwise, qualified services. If advice is necessary, legal or professional, a practiced individual in the profession should be ordered.

In no way is it legal to reproduce, duplicate, or transmit any part of this document in either electronic means or in printed format. Recording of this publication is strictly prohibited and any storage of this document is not allowed unless with written permission from the publisher. All rights reserved.

Table of Contents

- INTRODUCTION 1
- SEASON 1 6
- HIRE YOURSELF AND BE YOUR OWN BOSS 6
  - Taking Charge towards Becoming Your Own Boss 6
  - Creating Yourself and Becoming Your Own Boss 7
- SEASON 2 11
- OWNERSHIP OF BUSINESSES 11
  - Starting a Business 11
  - Buying an Established Business 16
  - Be a Shareholder 19
- SEASON 3 20
- OWNERSHIP OF REAL ESTATES 20
  - What makes Real Estate special? 25
  - Buy Real Estate for Less than its worth 25
  - Allow an infinite investment return 25
- SEASON 4 27
- OWNERSHIP OF STOCKS 27
  - Types of Stock 28
- SEASON 5 31
- TEACH AND PROVIDE VALUE TO OTHERS 31
  - The secret to Using your skill to teach and earn money 31
- SEASON 6 35

SIDE HUSTLE AND PASSIVE INCOME	35
SEASON 7	38
BE A FINANCIAL INVESTOR	38
A LITTLE SOMETHING FOR THE ROAD	38
CONCLUSION	40

Introduction

Money is essential to living a life of abundance. We make money by providing value through jobs. It might sound strange but you can gain spiritual and emotional freedom by embracing those two seemingly materialistic ideas. It's essential that you master the worlds of money and work to enjoy the abundance you desire. But to do so, the behaviors and values you've acquired in the past need to be put aside.

In the significant poverty wars, capital has served both scholars and practitioners as the primary tool and chief foot soldier. If we deploy the right amount of effort at the right moment, the right things will happen, suffering will decrease, and misery will give way to happiness. Policymakers, business scholars, social entrepreneurs, and opinion leaders have suggested that combinations of factors are crucial for the world's poor to make significant gains. It is not enough to make more money to create wealth, but this is the most fundamental phase for those just starting out or in transition. Most of us have seen tables that demonstrate that a small amount saved and accumulated consistently over time will gradually add up to considerable wealth. But the other sides of the tale never cover specific techniques or approaches required from individuals to accumulate wealth.

Do you make enough in the first place to save? Bear in mind that you can only reduce costs by so much. You should look for ways to raise your income if your expenses are already cut down to the bone. Also, are you good enough at what you're doing, and do you love it enough to save sufficient funds or build financial pillars that will sustain you for 40 or 50 years?

Those starting their careers or changing their careers will determine how to derive their earned income from four factors by answering the following questions:

- What are you passionate about? You'll do better and be more likely to succeed in doing what you enjoy doing.

- What good are you at? Look at what you do well and how you can make a living with those skills.

- What's going to pay well? Look at jobs that can meet your financial needs if you invest your skills and passion in them.

- How to get to it? Determine the kind of schooling, training, and experience necessary to harness the options before you.

Taking these factors into consideration will place you on the right path. Being open-minded and constructive is essential. Fairly regularly, but at least once a year, you can also review your financial situation.

You're making enough money, living pretty well, just not saving enough. What's wrong? The primary reason this happens is that your expenses surpass your budget. Try these measures to build a budget or to get your current budget on track:

- For at least a month, chart your expenses. To help you do this, you may want to use a financial software/program. Make sure the costs are classified. Be mindful of how much you spend; this will help you curtail your spending habits.

- Trim the excesses. Break down your expectations and needs. Food, shelter, and clothing are necessities; these should be at the forefront before you consider your wants. For example, it might be normal for you to eat lunch daily at a restaurant. While this may not be a terrible thing altogether, twice or thrice a week, take your lunch to work, it will help you save money.

- Customize based on your changing needs. As you go along, you will typically find that a particular item has been over-budgeted or under-budgeted and that you need to change, do the needful.

- Get your cushion in place. You never know what's around the corner. The goal is to reduce expenses worth three to six months. This braces you for financial losses, such as a job loss or a health challenge. If it seems overwhelming to save this cushion, start saving little amounts.

The most crucial move is to differentiate between what you really need and what you only want. Finding easy ways to save additional money here and there could involve programming your heating system. Turning it down when you're not home, using standard instead of premium fuel, buying furniture from a quality thrift store, and learning how to cook.

This doesn't mean that all of the time, you have to be thrifty. You should be able to reward yourself and splurge (an acceptable amount) once in a while if you reach your savings target. You will feel better and be encouraged to make more cash.

In addition to saving, you could make profitable investments, such as your bank's savings account. That's good, huh? Wrong! If you want to build a sizable portfolio, you have to take on some risk, which implies you'll have to invest in securities. So, how can you decide what the correct exposure level is for you?

Start with an evaluation of your situation. To establish an investment strategy statement, the CFA Institute advises investors. Evaluate your return and risk threshold. Quantify all elements, including household income, timeframe, tax considerations, cash flow or liquidity requirements, and other factors that affect your financial life.

First, decide which asset allocation is suitable for you. Most certainly, unless you know enough to do something on your own, you would need to consult with a financial advisor. Your investment strategy should be the basis of this allocation. A mixture of cash, fixed income, equity, and alternative investments will most likely be included in your allocation.

Risk-averse investors should keep in mind that portfolios require at least some equity exposure to protect against inflation. Sometimes, younger investors can afford to commit more of their investments to equity than older investors because they have time on their hands.

Lastly, diversify. Invest in a variety of assets. Don't try to wait for the best time before you invest in the market. If one asset (i.e., large-cap growth) is underperforming the S&P 500, another is likely outperforming it. The timing factor is taken out of the game by diversification. A trained financial advisor will assist you in creating a prudent plan for diversification.

Season 1

Hire Yourself and Be Your Own Boss

Taking Charge towards Becoming Your Own Boss

You shouldn't make erratic decisions in the 21st century anymore. To live abundantly, you need to take care of your own destiny. You may think you're really in charge, but I bet you're still listening to others, whether they're your bosses, your clients, your consumers, or your distributors. Are you hoping for a raise or a new project or promotion? Are you awaiting payment, do you sit idly for clients to come to you or let you know about new goods from suppliers? In the twenty-first century, that won't cut it. You must become strategic and begin pathways of becoming your own boss.

The key to doing so is to break free of the victimization mindset that has taken over many people and conquers the doubts that retard your progress. You have to avoid blaming your condition on others, take full responsibility for your accomplishments and shortcomings, and take charge of your life. Maybe you've had stern parents or violent parents. Perhaps you believe that you are being discriminated against or you might be discriminated against. Frankly, these thoughts are not necessary. You're liable for your own success or failure. You are the only one that will be able to prevent you from becoming wealthy.

You have to wake up and appreciate life each and every day. You need to imbibe the attitude of accountability, be accountable for yourself. Understand that taking a chance doesn't imply gambling. You have to set goals and objectives to recognize that success is not unplanned. You should stop living in the past, start thinking about the future, and live your best life in the moment.

Creating Yourself and Becoming Your Own Boss

Typically, nine-to-fivers consider the thought of working for themselves as far-fetched and the stuff of dreams. On a lighter note, who wouldn't want to be a boss and have a few workers to boss around? But the thought of working and earning for yourself, doing what you have always thought of doing, and not having to play by the rules of the wants and desires of another is what we all secretly fantasize about, particularly on the days we despise our jobs. And, honestly, your business ideas could blossom into full-fledged companies with some planning and hard work.

Truth be told, when it comes to owning your own company in this ever-expanding world, there's too much you can do. So many entrepreneurs would recommend creating a "side business" when you are already working a full-time job to not place a burden on your finances. Businesses often need time to expand, so you can also be your own boss without having to work for other people. Start little, identify your passion, and channel the energy you use at work into your passion, and you would see that it will produce the desired outcome. Although it can be challenging to run your own business, note that it's worthwhile and can be achieved.

Transform your hobbies into a business: We don't need to go into businesses on the strength of our educational qualifications. Business ideas can also come from our hobbies. You might love cooking leisurely; this skill monetized and used to start a business.

Using all the opportunities available: Skills you have acquired over time from schooling and various forms of training can also be translated into business ideas. To become a business owner, brainstorm, and leverage your skills. Even the most straightforward business ideas come from what you already know.

It cannot be overemphasized to use the idea you already have. We all have a passion for different things. Look inward and look for that thing/business that thrills you. The following are the ideas you can consider to secure your financial future;

Sell tailor-made cakes: Do the job that makes you smile. Make beautiful birthday cakes and put smiles on people's faces. Get paid to do that also.

Become a handyman: Are you an Engineer and you are treated like trash at work? Don't be upset. You can show your skills by being a plumber or electrician and get paid steadily with little or no stress.

Become a niche travel agent: Instead of generalizing what you do, you could make yourself stand out by becoming a niche travel agent for people and earn money.

Create handmade jewelry: A lot of people love making things. They are so creative to the point that creating jewelry is their forte. It might be yours too. The world is rapidly changing, and people want to see what you can bring to the table; what you have 'upstairs' matters a lot. So, if you love jewelry and you know how to make them with your hand, this is for you.

Sell cookies: Are you fascinated by chocolate, mixing, and watching yourself create beautiful cookies? If you do, then this is yours. You can make and sell cookies for weddings, dinner parties, and make a fair amount of money. This idea could even lead to a full-fledged company.

Offer homemade packed lunch service: Those who have skills of knowing the foods that would reduce obesity or dishes that generally make the skin healthy, this is for you. You can lunch packs and sell them to people. They refer you, and you get more money.

Start a catering business: People who already work in a kitchen or went to cooking school could open their own catering business, do not waste your skills. Cook mouth-watering dishes and get paid for your work.

Freelance as a graphic designer: If you spend most of your time designing logos and stickers, people would love to pay for that.

Become a freelance writer: Have you sent a million proposals to various companies and have gotten no response? You can become a freelance writer from the comfort of your home. Being a freelance writer gives you some sort of freedom. Write for different people and get paid immediately.

Do portraits: Do you have an eye for art? Do you just sit and make portraits of various items? Don't make your skill go to waste. Sell beautiful portraits and make money from them.

Make and sell seasonal decorations: Do you love Christmas and have great business ideas for creating seasonal decorations? Make famous Christmas ornaments and get paid for it.

Become a voice-over artist: Are you bold and aren't nervous by the thought of singing or speaking in public? Start voice-over gigs and upload them to various social media platforms.

Become a pet-toy seller: Love to make pet-toys? Sell them online today and make money from them.

Season 2

Ownership of Businesses

Starting a Business

The first step in owning a business is to build one of your own. Starting a business means you are in charge, and you have the authority to manage the business whatever way you choose and start making money.

If you love to create things, love to start from scratch, and you want to gain experience running your own company, then you are ready to build your own business. Your time and resources would be needed for this journey. If you know you can deal with being alone and planning your business, you are on track already. It might be challenging, but the end is rewarding. These are some of the business ideas you can consider;

1. **Food Delivery**

The business of food delivery is now in vogue. Since the sector has broad national brands, your distribution company can specialize in certain areas.

2. **Kiosks for Food**

Food kiosks are a must, whether at an outdoor mall, sports venue, parks, or any location which attracts large groups of people. Running a food kiosk could be as simple as selling ice water, juice, and frozen foods. This business pays a lot, and you are guaranteed to get clients when the business is correctly located and offers goods at affordable prices.

3. **Fast-food Business**

Fast-food companies sell food quickly to customers at affordable prices. Such restaurants offer service in both drive-through and conventional sit-down setups.

This business is very successful because it delivers tasty food in a fast, low-cost way. Establish a fast-food company, and you can have an inexpensive place for people to eat, stay energized, and feel satisfied.

You should consider running a fast-food company if you are looking for a way to make customers happier, meet cravings, and provide people with the nourishment they need. For those who love making and serving tasty food that people at all income levels will enjoy, fast food restaurants are perfect. A successful food business has the potential to boost the mood, happiness, and energy levels of both those in your neighborhood and those traveling through the area.

4. **Popcorn Store**

7 Seasons Of Income

A lot of popcorn is consumed by people everywhere. They come in several flavors. Gourmet popcorn shops produce popcorn, ranging from popular flavors (e.g., chocolate, caramel, cheddar, etc.) to exotic ones (e.g., Oreo, Buffalo wing, etc.). Who does not like the delicious taste of popcorn? Create that business and watch yourself earn more than you imagined. Anyone with skills who is imaginative and enthusiastic about popcorn will enjoy running a gourmet popcorn store. Although making popcorn is a simple and easy process, it takes ingenuity to come up with tasty and original varieties.

5. Grocery Stores

Grocery shops sell catering and other household goods. Sometimes known as supermarkets, grocery stores are go-to outlets for the nutritional requirements of a household. They also sell basic kitchen utensils, disposable goods, cleaning supplies, sweets, beer, beverages, and items for self-care. Today's grocery stores are fantastic spots for specific household items.

A grocery store can be opened by any person who loves management of a point-of-sale job. The supermarket industry is tough, but there is undoubtedly a shot for those who have the talent for sales, capital-intensive business strategies, or retail plans. The founder of a grocery store should understand food very well and be excited about having the best food in the region.

6. International Food Stores

Foreign food stores are stores that sell imported food, they are also called international grocery stores. These foreign goods vary. Meat, snacks, alcohol, sweets, and condiments, are typically stocked in foreign food stores — items such as toys and cooking tools are also part of international stock goods.

For any business owner who enjoys exotic cuisine, the foreign food business is an excellent one that pays well. There is a great taste for salads, burgers, picnic lunches, specialty drinks, cakes, and prepared meals for the perfect international food store owner. The director at a foreign grocery shop is typically able to recognize the ethnicity of numerous foods. Usually, deli-lovers, bakers, and coffee operators are fine foreign food customers.

7. Restaurant

This type of business provides prepared meals and drinks and caters to clients who do not want to cook or enjoy the feeling of eating out. Some restaurants specialize in one kind of food, such as Italian or Mexican, whereas other restaurants, such as diners, offer general American food. The competition depends solely on the type of restaurant, the definition of a restaurant, and the average price per item on the menu.

A restaurant is a fast-paced enterprise to manage and is very challenging. As such, it is more ideal for individuals with exceptional leadership abilities and entrepreneurs who are excited about food. Restaurateurs also lead a busy lifestyle, so you must be ready to work and get a steady income all the same.

8. B&B or Hotel

Tourists would like to sleep anywhere that offers them comfort. Major hotel chains are always pricey and catchy. Besides that, the tourist will be keen to catch on the tradition of locals, have a proper fried breakfast, and an accommodation owner who not only knows the city but the people who live there. A lot of people pay large amounts of money to stay days in hotels. Start your own hotel business, fill this gap and earn good money.

9. Nightclub or Pub

An exciting way to make a living is to own or run a pub or club. With the option of ales or a menu of local specialties, there are still several opportunities that will make you stand out from the crowd; such an outlook draws visitors to a restaurant. With specialist DJs willing to 'shut down' the arena with a large crowd, clubs will make a name for themselves with their live music as well. I mean, who doesn't love going out with friends to a club they know they would have fun? Open a nightclub, give people a good time, and make money.

10. Starting your own line of clothes

You will get your clothes firm off the ground if you have any ideas in mind and a little bit of time on your hands.
You can set up your own clothing collection using Oberlo, Printify, Printful, or a similar fabric sourcing software if you already own a Shopify store. Each links the store to fashion printers and garment factories automatically. They also oversee every stage of the way of retail distribution for you, allowing you

to plan and effectively distribute a wide variety of items. You can make money through this from the comfort of your home.

Buying an Established Business

This isn't as easy as it looks. For those that cannot build their own businesses, you can buy an existing company and become its new owner. You receive complete control, but you'll have to work using its current operations initially. If the corporation already runs smoothly, there is nothing tasking you'll have to do.

It is less expensive to buy an existing business if it has proved itself to be successful. Here are websites to help you find the right company if you're interested in purchasing a business.

1. **BizBuySell.com**

BizBuySell.com says that it is "the best sales marketplace business on the platform." It provides customers with options for purchasing a business or franchise, selling a business, getting assistance with finance, and more. Users are able to browse by group, state, and region for corporations. They can set a minimum and maximum price, search for franchises by form, state, and the amount of cash you need to spend. The opportunity to scan for a company broker near you is another beneficial aspect of the website.

2. **BizQuest.com**

Users will search companies and franchises for sale by province, top towns, popular businesses for purchase, and popular restaurants for sale with BizQuest.com. BizQuest also provides incentives for vendors, including the publication of adverts posted on the affiliate websites of the organization, such as The Wall Street Journal and The New York Times. On this website, users can also locate a broker.

3. **BusinessBroker.net**

BusinessBroker.net has far more than 30,000 sites for business-for-sale. Users will look for companies and franchises on the website, locate brokers, and make searches by business and location. There is also a finance and loan center at BusinessBroker.net that provides technical assistance to guide you through your business financial options.

4. **BusinessesForSale.com**

Currently, in the United States and around the world, this platform has more than 73,000 business directories, including available franchises. In order to locate a company appropriate for their interests and preferences, consumers can browse by market area, venue, and business conditions, such as "work from home" or "owner-financed." For those in need of accountants, agents, and attorneys, BusinessesForSale.com also provides services such as email updates and a service list.

5. **BusinessMart.com**

BusinessMart.com offers both corporations and franchises, as well as tools and programs to assist with financing. Clients can browse by location and by type of sector. Users skilled in franchises would be able to check for sufficient capital. Ad listings that attract thousands of customers are provided by BusinessMart.com. In addition, the site helps prospective customers and small business owners to collect offers for services such as telecommunications systems and credit card processing from suppliers to help their businesses expand.

There are many others like these; you can find a lot on Google that would help you in making decisions when considering buying businesses.

There are different ways to buy businesses;

Get a franchise

For those who do not have the expertise or don't have time to learn how to run a company, having a business franchise is beneficial. Although this is the costliest of all potential choices, according to reports, it nevertheless has the best rate of success. Because what you get is a time-tested business model of goods and services that are market-validated. In addition, as a business partner, mentor, and consultant along the way, the franchisor will be there to help you.

A widespread misunderstanding is that to purchase and run a profitable franchise, you need to have previous experience in business (marketing, banking, etc.). It's not the case here! In reality, many franchisees have little to no experience in the industry or training.

Although getting business experience definitely helps, to start up a shop, you do not need to spend thousands of dollars on a business degree.

So, you might consider any of the following franchises if you're fascinated by the thought of owning your own franchise.

- **McDonald's**

    When you invest in this franchise, you would get popularity, brand recognition, and huge income.

- **Dunkin'**

This business is one of the most recognized in more than 30 countries. Buy into Dunkin' Donuts and get all the support and money you need to acquire wealth.

- **Taco Bell**

Another popular franchise which has been around for 50 years now; they offer their franchisees all the restaurant resources they need.

There are many others like Wendy's, Great Clips, RE/MAX, and the UPS Store. The secret is to look for the brand that fascinates you; then make the move to own one.

Be a Shareholder

While this is most commonly described as an acquisition, it is another way of becoming a business owner. As a small investor, though, you would have very little or no influence over the company's activities. Purchasing a company's shares in the stock exchange can easily be achieved. You only need to open an account with a stockbroker, invest money, and you become the part-owner of a publicly-traded company. Investing your assets in the stock market is a reasonable financial decision if you lack the time and sufficient business funds.

Season 3

Ownership of Real Estates

More than any sector, real estate has produced more wealth, but individuals remain cautious about coming on board. They often feel they must begin with large sums of money, this not always the case. Even if you're just starting out, if you understand what you're doing, you will make money from real estate.

That said, in real estate, there are various ways of making good money. The plan you adopt depends on whether you want to earn a passive income or an active income.

These are the different ways to generate income in real estate:
1. **Rentals**: Leveraging long-term buy-and-hold residential rentals is one of the most common strategies for earning cash in real estate. People need a place to live at all times. Adopting this method means that you will be involved in

renting property. To acquire your land, you need to exercise due diligence by identifying an ideal location. Once you do, it's Money, Money, and Money. When you're seeking long term residential rentals, secure very good locations. The area is more important than the property's current state. In reality, one of the best acquisitions you can make is run-down homes in fantastic locations. In the real estate industry, this requires a more conventional approach to earning profits. It involves renting a home to make a down payment and some cash on hand and only keeping the property in the long run. You can quickly get the property with a very low or even no down cost, depending on your personal circumstances. If this is a property with high income-generating potential, such an approach is sensible. If a residential rental has good cash flow, it might be a perfect investment.

2. **Real Estate Investment Groups (REIGs):** Real estate investment groups (REIGs) are perfect without the hassles of running it with those who wish to buy rental real estate. A capital buffer and access to finance are needed to invest in REIGs. Small mutual funds invested in rental properties are like REIGs. A firm owns or builds a series of apartment blocks or condos in a traditional REIG, and then encourages buyers to purchase them through the company, thereby becoming a part of the group. A single owner may own one or more units of self-contained living space. Still, all the units, maintenance handling, advertisement of openings, and interview of tenants are jointly handled by the organization running the investment. You can earn monthly income by making this investment in return for performing these management activities.

3. **Raw land Income**: Companies can pay you handsomely in royalty for any discovery or daily fees for facilities they install, based on your rights to the land. This includes jacks for pumps, pipelines, gravel pits, access roads, and cell towers. It is also possible to lease raw land for cultivation, typically agriculture. Land tracts of trees can be useful for timber, which can be harvested frequently.
4. **Residential property income**: The overwhelming majority of revenue from residential property comes in the form of rent. Your renters pay a monthly rent, which will rise with inflation and demand, and you take your expenses out of it, retaining the remaining portion as rental income.
5. **Commercial properties income**: Commercial properties may generate revenue from the above outlets, as rent again, but may also add one more in the form of option revenue. Many commercial tenants will pay premiums for lease options, such as the next-door office's right of first refusal. Tenants pay a fee to keep these replacements, whether or not they exercise them. For raw land and even residential property, options for large income often occur.
6. **House Flipping**: House flipping is for persons with extensive expertise in the appraisal, marketing, and restoration of real estate. House flipping requires money and the willingness, if necessary, to do or supervise repairs. This is the symbolic 'wild side' of investment in real estate. Real estate flippers are distinguished from buy-and-rent landlords, much as day trading is separate from buy-and-hold buyers. Real estate flippers also look to profitably sell the undervalued assets they purchase in less than six months as a case in point. Simple land flippers also do not participate in property improvement.

Therefore, to turn a profit without any changes, the transaction must already have the inherent value required, or they would remove the property from contention. Flippers who can't quickly unload a property can run into difficulties because they generally don't keep sufficient uncommitted cash to pay for a property's long-term mortgage. By acquiring moderately priced properties and adding value by renovating them, you can make a lot of money as a house flipper.

7. **Buy and hold**: One of the most common methods of earning real estate money is this. There are a variety of ways to do this: you can purchase and rent a single-family house; buy a multi-family home and live in one of the units while renting the other units and getting paid monthly in the process, preferably to offset the mortgage and your own living costs. You could also buy a multi-family home and rent all the units, just run the property yourself or employ a maintenance firm to manage rental units, while you get paid steadily.

8. **Airbnb and vacation rentals**: While the COVID-19 pandemic has paused it for now, many travelers embraced this alternative to staying in a hotel. The demand for home-away-from-home rentals has gone off in recent years. Homeowners make money on a short-term basis by renting out a house or even just a bed, mainly if the property is in an area that is a well-known tourist destination. When the demand for such a rental will recover is uncertain. But should it pop back up, bear in mind that in some cities, short-term rentals are regulated and often even prohibited. Before listing a property on a website like Airbnb, VRBO, or HomeAway, review your area's bylaws. Also, make an in-depth analysis of what the

expenditure would look like for example, how much cleaning and sanitizing between visitors would amount to.

9. **Lease options**: Leasing options are agreements that give a renter a choice to purchase the rented property during or at the end of the rental period. You could complete the deal later at a lower, pre-set price if you lease with an option to buy in a bull real estate market where prices are rising, or make a good profit by selling your purchase rights.

10. **Short Sales**: Short sales include renting a house from a loan while the mortgagee is behind on loans. A time-consuming and challenging proposition could be short sales, but it is excellent to pay!

What makes Real Estate special?

You will consider all the benefits of buying real estate that does not appear in other approaches to investing if you are passionate about your investments and serious about making money.

Buy Real Estate for Less than its worth

For $75,000 or $80,000, houses worth $100,000 can possibly be found. For $700,000, some real estate valued at $1 million can be found. At $350,000, you can find other assets worth $450,000. Even if you have not yet paid the dealer, you can enter an agreement to purchase a property and manage it instantly. You then go to the closing and give the dealer an acceptable price between 30 and 100 days later. To purchase the estate, you borrow money, and then close it, and you own it.

Allow an infinite investment return

When you find a $1 million house for $500,000 and your credit history isn't perfect, some lenders will lend $500,000 to you for $1 million worth of real estate. They will hope you skipped a deposit so they could take over $1 million for $500,000 worth of a real estate.

These Lenders are called "Hard moneylenders." They do not focus on your credit when making their lending decisions; they care about the commodity, the property itself. If it is a 60 to 75 percent loan to value, they will lend the funds irrespective of your credit. There are several banks and mortgage firms that lend to bankrupt people, folks who have made late payments, have poor credit, etc. On these properties, they may still lend you 60 to 80% of the selling price. That's why, without investing your own money into the house, you can find $100,000 worth of property and get it for $75,000, then borrow that $75,000.

For $1,000 every month, you rent the property, and your deposit for the $75,000 you lent is $700 a month. You make some money per month even with all the expenses: insurance, taxation, vacancies, maintenance, and overhead. Let's assume that after covering all the bills, you make a $100 gain a month from the rent. You still spent nothing on the house. There's an endless benefit for you: $X for $0 invested.

Do you know that if you were buying shares, gold or making some other investment, this would not work? In real estate, you can have a massive profit on your investment. Your redemption investment is still unlimited if you make just $1 because of unexpected circumstances since none of your capital is invested.

Season 4

Ownership of Stocks

Investing in stocks is one of the easiest ways to create wealth, and it takes less commitment than you would expect. It doesn't mean investing regularly, being stuck to a computer screen, or wasting your days obsessing overstock prices to make money off stocks.

There are two ways to make money by holding equity shares: dividends and appreciation of capital. Dividends are payments from business earnings in cash. If a corporation has 1,000 shares in the hands of investors, and you buy a share, if the corporation declares a dividend of $ 5000, stockholders will get $5 for each share they own; you will be paid $ 5.

The appreciation of capital is the growth of the share price alone. If you sell a share for $10 to someone, and the stock is worth $11 later on, the shareholder makes $1. That being said, the benefits of investing in stocks are endless, and that is why stock investment has produced some of the billionaires we know in the USA, like Warren Buffett.

Types of Stock

Stock types are an essential part of the fund base for anyone looking to invest. The difference between various types of stocks needs to be understood by Investors. It is so important to know stock categories because it helps you understand each and to see the massive benefits to help you decide which you would be leaning towards. We have Growth Stocks and Value Stocks.

1. **Growth Stocks**

Some corporations do not like to pay their owners dividends. They would rather repay than disburse dividends to holders in their own businesses. This strategy guarantees more profit and dividends to a company's shareholders. Growth stock appreciates market shares, and because of that, it will make a huge income for you.

Growth stocks are an opportunity for a business to venture into the unknown while giving shareholders an advantage in the valuation of the shares. Very few of the stockholders are expected to collect their investment dividends. However, the money value of a company's stocks that perform well in their growth would be far greater due to the lack of concern.

When they ultimately sell their shares, a shareholder gets a huge payout and earns a lot of money from their investment.

They seem to have loyal customers or a significant market share in their industry due to their innovation patterns. For example, by gaining market share as the only company providing a new service, a business that develops computer applications and is the first to offer a unique service may become a growth stock, and a common (permit me to use) person comes in and buy the stock, his income is endless.

Some of the growth stocks you can make money from are PayPal, Etsy, Zoom, eBay, square, Wayfair, and many others.

2. **Value Stocks**

Value stock capitalizes on the fact that by acquiring low-priced shares in strong but temporarily unpopular firms, you will make money. This understanding will lead to tactics that are reasonably safe to enjoy stable returns. That being said, it is essential to become acquainted with the benefits of investing in value stocks. You will make a long-term profit investing in this stock.

You should consider investing in value stock if you want to make money. Though there is no guarantee on ordinary stock, dividends are paid on value stock, investing in value stock.

A few value stocks are undervalued simply because of low earnings reports or negative publicity from the media. Nevertheless, one attribute they often have is positive dividend-payout records. A stock of value with a strong dividend track record can provide an investor with reliable earnings. Many value stocks are older businesses that, even if they are not incredibly innovative or prepared to grow, they can be counted on to remain in business.

Investors buy value stock periodically for the sole purpose of collecting dividends. What are you waiting for? Invest in the stock business today and start accumulating wealth.

The value stocks you can generate wealth from are: Apple, McDonald's, Verizon, Berkshire Hathaway, Microsoft, AT & T, Starbucks, Tesla, Amazon, and many others.

Season 5

Teach and Provide Value to Others

The secret to Using your skill to teach and earn money

Do people still want to pick your brain? Do you waste hours weekly having coffee with individuals who wish to know how to do some of the things you are good at? Do they keep quizzing you on how to answer social media questions? It's nice to support people, but your time and experience are valuable. To monetize your skills, consider moving the lessons and tips you offer to a more formal stage. Here are a couple of ways you might do that.

1. **Make YouTube Videos** This is one of the lucrative ways to teach people and earn. Technology is good because it has made it easier to get paid while doing what

you love. Do you love teaching people or motivating them to do better? Are you witty and have an eye for comedy skits? Do you love cooking, and it just makes you happy? You can open a YouTube channel and make videos. People love to watch those. Just choose your favorite pastime, make videos of it, post them on YouTube, and start getting money from it.

2. **Create an Online Course**: You must have seen online courses taught by gurus get strongly promoted. Do you know that anybody can build an online course on any subject? Between a few hours to a 30-day period or longer, you can pick the duration that you want. It will help you get started with online class sites like Udemy, Skillshare, Braincert, or Teachable. This money-making gambit is hugely appropriate for those who are already making YouTube videos. The easiest way to market an online course is to get a wide audience on YouTube, Facebook, or a blog.

3. **Write an ebook**: Writing an ebook is the deal today. Choose a niche or topic that you feel is the trend today. For instance, people want to know how you can make money, so if you are experienced in this aspect, consider writing an ebook and selling it on Amazon or another website and earn an income from it. You can write as many until your ink runs dry!

4. **Host an art and wine party**: You've probably been invited to at least one party where adult cocktails are consumed as a teacher led you to make a simple drawing in oil or acrylic. You already have the skills required to teach one of these fun courses, whether you're an art

teacher trying to make money on the side or just an artist by hobby. At a paint-and-sip spot, you might get an instructor position or simply try hosting a party at home or in a rented room.

5. **Tutoring**: Are you well-read and love teaching students? You can earn a living from teaching. You could target the kids studying for SATs around you and tell them you'd tutor them well at an affordable price. Most parents want to see their children excel. Before you know it, you are getting good money from tutoring. You could also try out online tutoring. It's like being in the same room as the student. There are some tutoring websites such as Chegg and VIPKid that charge $20 per hour or more.

6. **Tour guide**: You can demonstrate your skill as a tour guide by providing guidance to large audiences from a day trek to a multi-week camping trip, whether your talent is kayaking, climbing, or trailblazing. For steadier work, freelance or link up with a tour company.

7. **Start a podcast**: If you are a professional in a specific area but would rather chat about it than write it down, your vehicle might be a podcast. These days, you can buy good quality microphones at good prices. If you don't know how to get started, you can take an online podcast launch course. You could also make money coaching people to podcast until you get the hang of it.

8. **Offer music lessons**: Some people know their music well. You could get paid for giving music lessons on YouTube too. Some people even go as far as teaching it

in school. They just show up for a couple of hours, teach and get a lot of money from it.

Other ways you can earn money from teaching are: coaching a sports team, teaching at a local community center, teaching a college course, and many more.

Season 6

Side Hustle and Passive Income

Passive income is desirable and often misunderstood. It takes a great deal of commitment and patience to grow sources of passive income. Revenue sources like these expand after the initial investment of hard work, and sustain themselves, giving you steady cash flow without much effort from you. The end justifies the means, right?

Here are some passive income ideas:

- **Self-publishing**: Currently, self-publishing is widespread. There's a pretty decent chance of owning a self-published book when you buy an eBook from Amazon. Self-publication is incredibly easy, as well. A few years back, I tried this and discovered how easy it was. You would first need to write and edit it, create a cover, and then submit it to a service like Amazon's Kindle Direct Publishing to self-publish your book. Don't expect results immediately. Before you can transform this into a passive income source, you'll need to make a lot of upfront ads.

- **Make a Copyright of your Music**: You can license and earn a profit from your music, much like stock pictures, anytime someone wishes to use it. Songs for YouTube videos, adverts, and more can also be copyrighted. There is more competition than ever for music, with the number of YouTube videos and podcasts made daily, and people are prepared to pay for it. The primary way to do this is to get the music to a library so people can look for it.

- **Build and Sell Apps**: if you have a smartphone or tablet, then it is fair to say that you have downloaded many applications. Have you ever come up with a fantastic idea for an app? If so, to make this come true, you should hire a programmer if you don't have programming skills. After building your software (app), you will market it for residual sales at the App store.

- **Affiliate marketing**: is the process of working with a corporation to earn a commission on a purchase, which means "becoming their affiliates." This approach to generating an income is suitable for people with blogs and websites.

- **Network Marketing**: It appears like network marketing, or multi-level marketing, is on the increase. Many of the multi-level marketing firms are Amway, Herbalife, Avon Products, Infinitus, and Mary Kay. By building a team below you referred to as a downline, you can gain passive income from network marketing. If you have a big team, you can earn commissions on their revenue without doing anything.

- **Drive for Uber or Lyft**: For Uber or Lyft, one of the easiest ways to make money is to drive. Today, the social economy is booming, with both Uber and Lyft at the top of the list. The finest part? With a simple click of a button, you can turn your availability on and off through these networks, allowing you to make money smartly regardless of the time.

- **Become a chef**: Are you an excellent cook? You can become a personal chef and cook meals for people. On social media, you might quickly sell your services or even go all out and create a website for yourself. There are also several blogs, such as HireAChef, that you can use to advertise your services.

- **Become a babysitter or part-time nanny**: You could babysit or even becoming a part-time nanny when you need to make some fast cash. To do this, you can use a range of apps, such as Care.com or SitterCity, or share your services on social media websites. You can get vetted and rated, so make sure you deliver top-notch service.

Other semi-passive ways to make income are selling vending machines, housekeeping, storage rentals, Laundromat, get paid for downloading apps, Cashback Sites, Rent Out Your Car, and many others.

Passive income is how the wealthy build their wealth. You should use your time and resources to harness business opportunities that can grow in the future if you don't have capital. You can use your money (and even combine it with your time) to produce more and more passive income as you go along.

Season 7

Be a Financial Investor

A little something for the road

1. **Financial Investor in Startups**: This is often the fastest way for an investor to make money. When a startup is purchased, the acquisition company may obtain cash or new stock (or a combination of the two) from an investor. How much an investor will receive from such a transaction or takeover depends on his share of the startup and the price at which the corporation was purchased.
2. **Financial Investor in Stocks, bonds, dividends**: Yeah, you will become a millionaire by trading in the stock market! In reality, the stock market is a place that, even when you are sleeping, it will help you produce tremendous wealth. Over time, the strongest firms appear to raise their earnings, and buyers compensate these larger profits with a higher stock price. Sufficient time on the

market also allows dividends, shares, and securities to be received.

3. **Financial Investors in Real Estates**: Investing in real estate has been discussed earlier can yield great profit. This investment comes in different ways; picking anyone would make you money.
4. **Financial investor in Businesses**: Whether you are starting up a business or buying an already established business, you can make a lot of money from investing in businesses like those mentioned above.
5. You can get a great deal from investing your time in teaching people. As mentioned above, you will need a stable internet connection, laptop, and commitment to see this through. By the end of the first month of whatever you are investing in, you will be surprised at the amount of money you are making.
6. A side hustle could make you huge money. You could go about other important activities in your life while making a steady income when you make your house available on a rental platform like Airbnb.

Conclusion

Now that you're ready to be your boss, you would need to make a schedule that covers your activities and goals annually. This is important to ensure your company runs smoothly. Your plan should cover daily, weekly and monthly benchmarks, and must be evaluated periodically.

This will allow you to make necessary adjustments and improvements when there are apparent shortcomings or in situations where demand exceeds supply. Delegating duties to employees would be helpful, so it's important that you get an assistant.

Many believe that it is difficult for ordinary citizens to get wealthy without an obscene degree of success at gambling or the lotto; we now know that such assertions are untrue. Others assume that it takes money to become wealthy. Some people also attribute financial success to hard work. Still, some opine that becoming wealthy is all about maximizing investment secrets and insider information.

The reality is that the components required to create considerable wealth are not far-fetched. They are around you, when harnessed; they can make the remainder of your life more comfortable. It would help if you like hard work, it would be better if you worked smart. You need to acknowledge your shortcomings, understand the factors responsible for your current financial problems and aim to make the most of the hand you're playing with.